How to Spend Less Without Being Miserable

Prentice Hall LIFE

If life is what you make it, then making it better starts here.

What we learn today can change our lives tomorrow. It can change our goals or change our minds; open up new opportunities or simply inspire us to make a difference. That's why we have created a new breed of books that do more to help you make more of *your* life.

Whether you want more confidence or less stress, a new skill or a different perspective, we've designed *Prentice Hall Life* books to help you to make a change for the better. Together with our authors we share a commitment to bring you the brightest ideas and best ways to manage your life, work and wealth.

In these pages we hope you'll find the ideas you need for the life *you* want. Go on, help yourself.

It's what you make it

* * *

How to
Spend Less
Without Being
Miserable

RICHARD TEMPLAR

Harlow, England • London • New York • Boston • San Francisco • Toronto • Sydney • Singapore • Hong Kong
Tokyo • Seoul • Taipei • New Delhi • Cape Town • Madrid • Mexico City • Amsterdam • Munich • Paris • Milan

PEARSON EDUCATION LIMITED

Edinburgh Gate
Harlow CM20 2JE
Tel: +44 (0)1279 623623
Fax: +44 (0)1279 431059
Website: www.pearsoned.co.uk

First published in Great Britain in 2009

ISBN: 978-0-273-72555-8

British Library Cataloguing-in-Publication Data
A catalogue record for this book is available from the British Library

Library of Congress Cataloging-in-Publication Data
Templar, Richard.
  How to spend less without being miserable / Richard Templar.
    p. cm.
  ISBN 978-0-273-72555-8 (pbk.)
  1. Shopping. 2. Consumer education. 3. Finance, Personal. I. Title.
  TX335.T396 2009
  381.3'3--dc22
                                    2009005371

10 9 8 7 6 5 4 3 2 1
13 12 11 10 09

Text design by Design Deluxe
Typeset in ClassicalGaramondBT-Roman by 30
Printed and bound in Great Britain by Clays Ltd, Bungay, Suffolk

The publisher's policy is to use paper manufactured from sustainable forests.

To Luke, who has mastered the art of living frugally and enjoying it

Contents

Introduction

I guess you've picked this book up because you know, however reluctantly, that it's time to tighten your belt. You may have been putting it off for a while, but now it's time to actually do something about it. But deep down you are worried about all this reining in and cutting down. After all, who wants to become a miserly, frugal penny-pincher depriving themselves of all life's little pleasures?

Well, the good news is that spending less doesn't have to make you miserable. In fact, you might actually start to quite enjoy some of it (trust me and hang on in there … I might just be telling you an unbelievable truth). You see, this isn't all about what you do. There are actions you can (and probably should) take, but the biggest changes will happen inside your head. You just need to think differently, change your attitude, alter your mindset. And I'll show you how.

There are lots of books that give you tips for cutting back, and websites to use to save you money, and some of those may be useful. But my real interest is in the way people think and behave, and the people I know who manage to live the most frugally seem to adopt a different approach to spending from the rest of us. And that means that they're happy to be thrifty because it doesn't go against the grain.

I have some experience of this myself. I can't pretend that I'm dirt poor these days. I'm lucky enough to be pretty comfortable, at least in a good year. But back in the '89 recession[1] I had to learn pretty much every strategy I could to keep the wolf from the door. I remember sitting at the kitchen table (I'd sold off most of the other furniture) with a pile of bills, sorting them into ones I could pay and ones I couldn't – and wondering what to do about the second, larger pile.

To begin with I hated it. Apart from the worry, I just hated having to go without things I was used to having. But at some point I underwent a kind of epiphany and I started to find it hugely liberating. It was nothing to do with how much cash was in my pocket – it was my attitude that changed. I suddenly reached a point where I found I could enjoy myself perfectly well on a far tighter budget.

I've included in here the lessons I learnt, along with many I've gleaned from watching and talking to other people. You'll find some of the most useful ideas I've discovered for keeping spending down, and you'll also find plenty of strategies for changing your way of thinking, because that's the most essential bit of all.

If there's one thing I've learnt over the years it's that how happy you are just doesn't correlate with how much money you have, at least so long as you stay above a very basic minimum level. I've known

[1] Yes, I was already grown up then ...

miserable millionaires and cheerful paupers. What makes people happy goes on inside their heads, not their wallets.

I've included 100 of the most important lessons for living frugally in this book, but I don't claim they're the only 100. If you have other ideas you think I've missed, or if you'd like to let me know whether this book has worked for you, I'm always interested to hear from you. You can email me at **Richard.Templar@RichardTemplar.co.uk**.

Richard Templar

You have to want to do it

This is perhaps the trickiest part of the whole money-saving thing. Of course, if you're even reading this, you'd *like* to have more money, or to see it disappear a little less quickly. And maybe the only way that's going to happen is by spending less. But in order for it to happen you have to move from 'wanting to want to' spend less, and get to a place where you really do 'want to'. I know that's confusing but I don't know a better way to explain it, and it's important. You have to really, really want to spend less. In other words; it has to go from being a nice idea in theory to a very strong desire which you're truly committed to deep in your heart and soul.

Let me give you an example. I have a friend who is in quite a sticky financial position. She has big credit card debts and is struggling to pay her bills. She says she desperately wants to cut down her spending. Last month she flew to New York for a friend's wedding, and bought herself a dress for $700 to wear to it.

Now I can see that my friend *wants to want to* spend less. But if she really wanted it fully in her heart of hearts, she'd never have bought that dress, and she probably wouldn't have gone to the wedding at all.

If you're in the same position, I can't wave a magic wand, I'm afraid. But I can tell you that you need to find the motivation truly to want to spend less. Where you find that motivation is up to you – it might be in the final demand from the water company, or in the letter summoning you to see your bank manager, or in your partner threatening to leave, or in something more positive such as the prospect of what you will do to celebrate when you manage to actually build up some savings, or how good you will feel when the debts start to disappear. But while you're busy looking for ways to save money that might work, you need to look even harder for the motivation to stick with it.

GET YOUR KICKS
SOMEWHERE
ELSE

D iversion tactics work brilliantly on kids, and they can work just as well on us. Well, we're only big kids ourselves really, aren't we? If you get a real kick out of spending money, perhaps you should find something else that gives you the same buzz. When you feel a shopping spree coming on, go for a run instead, or have a long pampering bath, or summon your partner for a session in bed, or whatever does it for you.

Certain diversions are out, of course – online gambling, expensive pampering therapies, or anything that involves spending more than you're saving. Similarly you don't want to create problems of equal proportions by taking up smoking or excessive drinking or overeating. However, that should still leave you plenty of choices.

You can learn to recognise what drives you to shop – are you more likely to overspend when you're depressed, or excited, or angry? Once you start to understand the tricks your mind is playing on you, you can start to recognise the danger signals and take avoiding action.

I should just add (if only to keep my publisher happy) that this book isn't intended to help people with a serious spending addiction; I'm not qualified to help you with this, and you really do need to get professional advice. Or at least buy a book that is aimed at helping you.

Know your budget

How much more (or less) do you earn than you spend? In other words, what's your available spending money?

How much do you owe – in bills you can't pay or in loans and credit cards that you're paying off over time?

How much of your money goes on household shopping? How much on regular bills, and which ones?

How much goes on the kids, from new shoes to swimming lessons?

How much goes on clothes, holidays, cars, decorating the house, gardening, Christmas shopping, socialising, hobbies?

Where does the rest of it go?

Listen, if you're serious about spending less you need to know exactly what you're spending now, what it's going on, and how much is left over – or under – at the end of the month. Sure, you can have some success with a bit of ad hoc money-saving here and there, but without a proper understanding of your own money you simply can't see where money is being spent unnecessarily, where there's most scope for saving, what you really need to spend, and so on.

So sit down with an old-fashioned pen and paper[1] and work out what money comes in, and what goes out, and where it goes. I can tell you that once you've done it you'll feel better just for having the answers to all those questions.

[1] The back of an envelope will do – no need to buy a new pad especially.

Remember
the glass is
half full

It's miserable having to spend less. All those things you have to go without, that you used to be able to afford. You're bound to feel negative, aren't you?

No, you're not. Come on, snap out of it. There are worse things in life, and people living on far less than you.[1] You just have to adopt a more positive approach. Don't think, 'I can't afford this,' think, 'I *can* afford that.'

Try finding a positive way to look at everything – make it a game if you like. Instead of thinking something is out of your price range, think, 'If I save up for long enough I can get that.' OK, you might have to save for months or years, and you might not want it enough for that – but that's positive too: 'I don't really need that anyway, I've got better things to spend my money on.'

If you're miserable, it's only because you choose to be. So don't go moaning about it. You can just as easily choose to be cheerful despite having to spend less. It takes a bit of practice but it gets easier as it goes on, and you can learn to enjoy yourself with or without money. Yes, really.

[1] There are even people out there who can't afford to buy this book.

SAVE
TIME

I t's a funny thing I've noticed, but the people who manage to live happily on less money tend to be the ones who have the most time. I guess that's because we often spend money in order to save time – taxis, ready-meals or whatever. So it follows that if you don't need to save the time you won't need to spend the money.

People with less time are the ones who drive rather than walk, who never cook their own food, who employ a cleaner, who pay a childminder, who run expensive cars and have to get the garage to fix every little problem.

So if you can find ways to free up time (and yes, before you write in, I know that can be very difficult) you can use that extra time to cut down on your spending. Some of the money-saving options you'll free up you may hate, but others you may really enjoy. Personally I prefer driving to walking more than about half a mile (except when I'm walking the dog). On the other hand, I quite enjoy cleaning and I love having time to cook and to spend with the kids.

The most important thing is to recognise the equation that less time = less money, so the more time you commit in various ways, the more expensive your life is likely to be.

If you need some time-saving ideas, look out for my companion book to this one, *How to Get Things Done Without Trying Too Hard*.

GET
ORGANISED

Here's another thing that doesn't immediately look relevant but actually couldn't be more so. You'll find that people who are organised spend less (on average, obviously) than unorganised people.

Think about it. If you leave it until the last minute to book your train tickets, you'll have missed all the discount special-saver super-advance tickets and you'll have to pay full fare. If you don't post your Christmas cards until the last possible moment, you'll have to pay first-class postage to get them there on time. If you haven't taken out the pet insurance you need and your dog breaks a leg, it will cost you a fortune. If you don't get round to fixing the leak in the roof, you'll end up having to replace the rotten joists as well as the tiles.

I'm not going to lecture you here because the kettle might object to me calling it black, but I do know that when money is tight, being organised stops being a luxury to aspire to and becomes a necessity. I know how painful it is to become organised when it doesn't feel natural, but I promise you it will pay for itself – literally.

SEE IT AS A
CHALLENGE

One of the best ways to enjoy a budget lifestyle is to really get stuck into the challenge of seeing how much money you can save, where the best bargains are, what you can do without, how you can cut back further. You could turn into a real bore on the subject of which supermarket sells the cheapest butter, or how much petrol you can save by taking a different route to work. And why not? If everyone else is bored, that's their problem. Go on – have fun sending them all to sleep.

Why not keep an eye on your weekly or monthly outgoings and see if you can't reduce them every time? It will probably be pretty easy to begin with but, like all good challenges, it will get harder as it goes on. But you can do it. In a few months' time you'll find the only way to keep spending less than the previous week or month will involve arranging carshares or making the Sunday roast feed the family all week. A few months after that you'll be living on roadkill but, hell, you'll be enjoying yourself.

Make bargain-hunting a hobby

If you make bargain-hunting fun, and learn to relish finding products at a fraction of what you'd pay elsewhere, you can turn frugal living into a thoroughly enjoyable way of life. You can get a real high from buying at a knock-down price, not to mention the buzz you get from bragging about it later. (Well, why not? You've 'earned' the right.)

I knew one woman who was really struggling as a mother-of-three who encountered hard times and was finding it very difficult just to afford the essentials. But being of an amazingly positive disposition, she just got stuck into the challenge of making ends meet, no matter what. She found she enjoyed it so much that she ended up making a nice little bit of money on the side buying and selling antiques and collectibles. Eventually this turned into a very respectable business – and that was before the days of eBay and online selling. She still does it well into her 70s – not because she has to, but because she simply loves doing it.

KNOW WHEN A BARGAIN IS NOT A BARGAIN

I've had a number of arguments with my wife on this particular point, which she has regrettably won. I know she's right[1] so I'm passing it on, and I can also empathise with anyone who is reluctant to take this lesson on board. In order to explain this, I have only to tell you how the conversation goes:

ME: 'Look at this! What a bargain.'

MY WIFE: 'That's not a bargain.'

ME: 'Yes it is, look – it's half price. Only a fiver.'

MY WIFE: 'You don't actually *need* one of those.'

ME (*hopefully*): 'Yes, I know. But it's so cheap … such a bargain …'

MY WIFE (*sighing*): 'We've been here before. It's *not* a bargain. It may be £5 less than it usually is, but it's still £5 more than you need to spend. You aren't saving a fiver. You're *spending* a fiver.'

Enough said.

---

[1] It goes without saying that you're not to tell her that.

HOARD YOUR
SAVINGS

No, I'm not talking about keeping all your worldly cash under your pillow. What I mean is that you can motivate yourself to save money by keeping the money you've saved where you can see it. Suppose you manage to give up smoking, or to cut down on your alcohol consumption, or to spend less on food. Instead of leaving the money you've saved in your bank, or wallet, or wherever you like to keep it, put it somewhere visible instead.

I like to keep a jar of loose change in my living room. I empty out my pockets most evenings and put all the coppers and shrapnel in there. You'd be surprised how quickly it adds up. Whether it's loose change or the savings from cutting back that you're collecting, you can actually see what you're achieving. That makes it much more fun and gives you a feeling that it's worth the sacrifice. Once or twice a year you can take it to the machine at your local supermarket, or to your bank, and swap it for more usable notes. You can comfortably save a healthy three-figure sum in a year this way.

Sooner or later you may want to do something with this money, or there's not much point having it. Either you can put it towards something you really need or, if you can manage without it and can afford to save it, you can always allow yourself a modest share of it – say, 5 or 10 per cent – to spend on yourself. Set this proportion before you start so you're less tempted to exceed it, and then enjoy yourself with it. You deserve it.

Try an
alternative
savings
scheme

Here's a technique that a friend of mine uses very successfully, and which I think is really smart. She uses it most often for buying clothes, but as you'll see you can apply it to any non-essential spending.

If you see anything you really want to buy but can't afford, save for it by not buying other things you normally would. For example, you might walk rather than take the bus or tube, maybe take egg sandwiches into work for lunch instead of buying sandwiches out, or you might give up alcohol, eat at cheaper restaurants than usual, not go to the cinema and so on.

Keep a tally of the money you're saving so you know when you've 'earned' enough to buy the thing you want. You'll enjoy it so much more than if you'd bought it straight off and then fretted over your bank statement.

LOOK FOR
CHEAP THRILLS

There are lots of inexpensive ways to socialise, and plenty of them can be really good fun. In fact, just coming up with them can be rewarding in itself. Anyway, it's good for you to do something different for a change; it keeps your mind fresh. As my old English teacher would have said, 'It's good for the soul.'

So forget going down the pub on a summer evening, and persuade some of your friends to go for a walk instead or arrange to meet on a scenic hilltop. You can always take a hip flask or a picnic supper and you can still make sure you save money. In fact, why limit it to those light summer evenings? If the weather is tolerable you can have huge fun scaring each other with ghost stories on a winter's night out on the moors or down in the woods or wherever your local beauty spot happens to be.

I've had romantic dinners in restaurants, but I've had equally enjoyable fish-and-chip suppers down by the river, eating out of the paper the fish came wrapped in. I've had some great evenings out at the theatre, but the local bowling alley is a thoroughly entertaining venue for a night out too.

Set yourself a two-part challenge. Part one, inject a bit of variety into your social life, and part two, make sure it's less expensive than whatever you'd normally be doing. If you need any more incentive, get together with your partner or a friend and see who can come up with the cheapest thrill.

Give yourself a cooling-off period

This is especially useful to follow if you're prone to impulse buys. Make a rule that you won't buy anything until you've had at least a day to think about it. Obviously this doesn't apply to things like the weekly food shop, or you'd end up fasting for a day every week – although, mind you, that would help you spend less. But it makes sense for anything non-essential, whether it's a car or a new saucepan or a pair of trousers or a squirrel trap.[1]

I buy quite a lot by mail order (I live in the back of beyond) and when you look through catalogues it's easy to be tempted by all sorts of things you didn't really pick up the catalogue to look for. However, if I mark the pages and then wait a week, I find that I end up changing my mind about most of them and I really don't struggle to decide against them. I don't even think, 'I'd love to, but I just can't afford it.' What I actually think is, 'What on earth did I put a marker in that for?'

[1] Well, I don't know what you like to spend your money on.

Imagine
yourself
without it

ere's a quick trick that I find really useful when looking at yet another overcoat (I love overcoats). I imagine how I'll feel if I go out of the shop without buying it. Will it eat into my brain for the next few days? Or will I have forgotten all about it in an hour or so?

Almost invariably, I reckon I'll forget about the thing. So I have a rule that if I can possibly resist it, I will. And you know what? I *can* resist when I think of it like that.

And anyway, if it is still eating into my brain in a week's time I can always go back for it. It's never happened yet.

PUT IT AWAY
BEFORE YOU
GET IT

I t's far easier to save money you've never had, than to take money out of your wallet or account and transfer it to savings after you've seen that nice fat wad of notes, or that healthy balance.

I have a friend who has set up a direct debit so that the very day her salary arrives, a certain amount is immediately transferred to her savings account. This way it never shows up in her current account, and she isn't tempted to spend what she thinks she doesn't have. Brilliant in its simplicity. I know another chap who does this with every pay rise. He's still living on what he earned in 1989 but hell, it paid for his wedding among other things.

If like me you're freelance and your earnings aren't regular, this is trickier of course. But if you know when a certain payment is going into your account (maybe you just paid the cheque in today and are waiting for it to clear), you can still set up a one-off transfer to your savings account for as soon as the money reaches your current account.

Ringfence funds

You know those big tax and utility bills that you try to bury your head in the sand about? The ones you know perfectly well are coming, but you'd rather not think about them? Well, wouldn't it be nice not to have to worry about them because the money was already there? In the good times, you can always scrape together enough to pay them, but just now you may really struggle.

So set aside a certain amount every time money comes in, so that when the bill comes you can feel self-satisfied – yes, even smug. You know roughly how much the bill is likely to be, so that's the amount to set on one side. The best way is to set up another account altogether to keep the money in – even at a different bank if that helps psychologically to keep it apart and not be tempted to dip into it.

This works not only for bills but for any other large expenditure that you suspect you may not have the money for when the time comes. That means holidays, Christmas, your wedding – whatever you want to be sure to have the funds to cover. You can open separate accounts for these, although I don't recommend trying to run a dozen different accounts.

And why not make it a higher-rate savings account while you're at it, and make yourself a bit more money in the process?

USE BIG
MONEY

When was the last time you cracked a fiver? You probably can't remember, it's such an everyday thing to do. How about the last time you broke into a £50 note? That's far more memorable – OK, you might not recall the exact occasion, but you'll have noticed it at the time.

So here's an idea. When you draw cash out of the bank, ask for the largest denomination notes you can get (obviously you'll have to go into the bank to do this – the cashpoint isn't going to give you an option). You'll think a lot harder about using a £50 or even a £20 note. Not only is it more inconvenient to change, but you really notice how the money is going down. You'll find you stop and think twice about what you're spending when it means cracking a £50 note.

SAY NEVER NEVER TO THE NEVER NEVER

I f you never borrow money, you can't get into debt. It's that simple. Back in my parents' and grandparents' day, you wouldn't dream of owing money. If you didn't have the money for something, you didn't buy it. End of story.

These days the banks practically throw credit cards at us, and there are ads everywhere for loans of one kind or other. But we don't have to play their game. We can always say, 'Thanks but no thanks.' You don't need a credit card if you have a debit card, and you don't need a loan at all. I make an exception here for mortgages, by the way. I will permit you to buy a house without getting told off for not saving up the full amount first.

If you were brought up in this mindset, you'll probably find it relatively easy. If you weren't, it's harder to get into the swing of it. Harder, but still perfectly possible. People who follow this approach rigorously will tell you that borrowing money would make them feel far worse than going without does. And of course not only does it mean you spend less, but you also save the cost of the loan.

THINK
GREEN

The basic mantra of being eco-friendly, green, environmentally aware, a tree-hugging hippy or whatever you like to call it, is 'reduce, reuse, recycle'. The crochet-your-own-wholewheat-pasta brigade[1] really do know a thing or two about living on the cheap.

Whether you really want to be green, or whether you'd just quite like to be if it's not too much effort, you'll find that there's a huge overlap between the green approach and the thrifty one. The 'reduce' part of the green slogan not only means reducing what you use but also thereby what you spend. Read a couple of green magazines[2] and start picking up a few tips. Before you know it you'll be making your own household cleaners from vinegar and bicarb (apparently both cheap and effective), getting and giving through freecycle.org and putting your babies into reusable cloth nappies.

[1] It's OK, no need to worry about offending them – they won't be reading this. They don't need it.
[2] Obviously don't buy them – reuse someone else's copy.

SELL THINGS

When I hit the rocks back in the '89 recession, I started selling things. I know this sounds obvious but there's a strange mental block you have to get over. If it's not something you normally do, you just don't see the possibilities. Once you start, however, you find you can sell all sorts of things you never noticed you didn't need. Personally, I found it hugely liberating.

There are lots of options once you decide to sell. One friend of mine realised he never really used the piano any more since his kids left home, and sold it to a friend with younger kids who he knew was interested. I used to sell my car and buy a cheaper one every so often (until I downgraded so far there really wasn't anywhere to go – at least not if I wanted a car that went).

Then there are local free ad papers, eBay and plenty more outlets. Car boot sales are great because you can offer to sell things for other people and take a cut, as well as selling off your own assets.

You can always promise yourself a modest treat once you've sold what you can, or allow yourself a small percentage of your takings as personal commission, while the rest gets saved or goes towards bills.

Be a
barterer

Just because you want to acquire something, it doesn't automatically follow that cash has to change hands. You can always swap goods or services instead. I know lots of people who do this informally – writers who will write a press release for an entrepreneur friend, or a tricky letter to an employer for someone, in exchange for a lawnmower or an evening's babysitting. I know someone who dog walks for a neighbour in exchange for them fixing his car from time to time.

There are also more formal systems set up which you might want to use. These are known as LETS (Local Employment and Trading Systems), which create their own currency. Each member has a cheque book and can 'buy' and 'sell' services from other members. No money changes hands, so it won't cost you anything (except a reasonable membership fee). If there isn't a scheme in your area, why don't you start one? You only need to get together a small group of local friends and neighbours to get it started. Google 'LETS' to find out how to set it up.

It stands to reason that bartering is going to work best if you have something other people want to buy. Whether it's home-grown vegetables, plumbing skills or time to walk the dog, you need to give as well as to receive.

GET ONLINE

Before we go much further, you're going to find that a lot of the ways of spending less in this book only work if you have online access. So if you're one of those people who doesn't yet have a computer, now's the time to invest in one. If you go for something basic it will pay for itself in no time so long as you take advantage of the many ways in which it can save you money. Ideally get one second hand – some gadget freaks upgrade when their old PC is perfectly up-to-date and fit for years' more use. All the better for you.

There are all sorts of hidden, secret ways of cutting down your spending that are known only to those who have access to the Internet.

So go and get yourself online if you're serious about spending less, and enrol on a course if you need help learning how to use the Internet. You may even be able to get free training if you look for it and ask around.

Don't
window shop

If you don't know it exists, you can't want it. It's really as simple as that.

Window shopping seems to be a national pastime, especially during times of recession. The thinking is that if you can't buy you can at least look. But actually you're just making it worse for yourself. Whether it's down at the shops, online or in mail order catalogues and magazine ads, if you see it, you'll want it. As Oscar Wilde said, 'I can resist anything, except temptation.'

So if you can't resist temptation either, avoid it instead.

Carry cash

When I say carry cash, that's only half the story. The other half is don't carry anything *except* cash. If you haven't got it, you can't spend it. OK, so I know this doesn't work online or over the phone, but it does work if you're going on a shopping trip in the real world – clothes, Christmas shopping, weekly supermarket shop, that sort of thing.

Decide in advance how much you can afford, get the cash out (in advance, obviously, because you won't have your cashcard with you when you go) and take nothing else with you. Now how are you going to overspend?

Clearly you have to apply some self-control when you're deciding how much to take with you. But that's easy because that's not where the temptation is. By the time you're actually out there, looking at all the things you could buy, you're already committed to staying within your budget.

DON'T PLAY WITH
PRETEND MONEY

Did you ever have toy money when you were a kid – probably with one of those plastic tills to go with it? Or did your kids? Well, that isn't real money, as you well know. That's pretend money.

But we grow up and we start living in the big grown-up world and we start using real money. We open bank accounts, and hand over real cash in shops, and write cheques. Then, around about the time we start to earn proper money, we get a credit card and feel like a real grown-up.

Wait! It seems like a logical progression from cash and debit cards and cheque books, but it's not. It's a regression to the toy money we had as kids. You see, when you hand over your credit card, you're not buying something with grown-up money. That money you're handing over *isn't real*. It's pretend money. Can you touch it? No. If you went down to your bank and asked for it, would they give it to you? No. Because it doesn't actually exist.

So do yourself a favour and stop playing with toy money. Stick to the real grown-up stuff and you'll be much safer.

FREEZE
YOUR
ASSETS

Here's a more permanent way to put the last two points into practice. It's ideal for anyone who can't trust themselves with plastic but can't get rid of it because of those odd occasions when it's really necessary.

Freeze your credit cards in a bowl of ice. That way you have them for utter emergencies (allowing time for thawing, of course) but they're no use for everyday spending.

Do your weekly shop online

Apologies if you live on a remote Scottish island or somewhere similar, but many of us now have the option of a supermarket home-delivery system.

There are plenty of advantages to shopping online for groceries. Once you get into the swing of it, it's much quicker (I grant you that it does start off a bit slower until you get your usual items listed). It also saves on your fuel costs, and is much more eco-friendly because only one vehicle is supplying loads of deliveries.

And it's cheaper for all but the most resolutely strong-willed. I know you may not believe me, but it's true. You see, it's easy to stick to your shopping list, whereas in a supermarket it's so hard when you spot a bargain here, or those juicy peaches over there, or smell that fresh-baked bread, or spot chocolate bars on a two-for-one offer.

I know you have to pay for the delivery – although this is cheaper on some days and at certain times, so try to plan round this – but I'll bet that it still costs you less overall, and you'll be wasting less food too.

NEVER SHOP FOR FOOD ON AN EMPTY STOMACH

Thiis is asking for trouble. If necessary, shove a slice of bread inside you on your way to the shops, but don't go shopping with a rumbling tummy or you'll want to buy everything you see.

Clearly online shopping is a very good way around this (it's still easier to do it on a full stomach). You may physically have to go to the shops to do your shopping, however, so aim to go after breakfast or lunch (or dinner if you really want to).

It also helps to identify aisles to avoid. Whether it's the biscuits or the alcohol, the chocolate or the frozen desserts, know where the danger spots are and make it a rule never to go down those aisles. If that means you have no way of gaining access to the tonic water or the frozen peas, well, go without those too. You'll save even more money.

SHOP IN
A HURRY

It stands to reason that if you have less time you'll buy fewer things. So make sure when you go shopping that you don't have time to browse for hours and spend money at leisure.

There are several ways of doing this. The most obvious is to have a deadline by which you have to stop shopping because you have an appointment or a school run. Or maybe you can park where you know you'll be clamped if you're not back before your money runs out. Another technique of mine, if I'm going to be shopping somewhere without a loo, such as a parade of shops, is to drink a litre of water before I go. That way I'm bound to have to head home before I've had time to spend all my money. If you have them, small children are an invaluable asset – you will be hassled out of the shop in no time, and have no chance of a leisurely browse.[1]

Of course you need to gauge the right amount of time to give yourself, but until you're practised at it I'd advise erring on the side of too little time rather than too much. This works as well for your weekly supermarket shop as for what you might call 'fun' shopping. After all, if you're up against the clock you'll only have time to buy what's on your list – no browsing the other aisles or getting distracted by offers on things you don't need.

[1] If you don't have small children, I bet you can find somebody to willingly loan you theirs for an hour with grateful thanks.

CUT OUT
COUPONS

I rritating little flimsy bits of paper – I hate them. Who wants to be forever cutting out stuff from magazines and remembering to take them to the shops? And who wants to be one of those infuriating customers who takes ages at the till handing the damn things over?

Well, if we've got any sense, we all do. Take a look at how much you can save on petrol alone if you actually use the coupons you get. And then there are all those other coupons the supermarkets give you, or that you find in magazines. I know it's a pain – I really agree – but it's a pain that's worthwhile.

Each individual token may save you only pennies (but hey, look after the pennies …) but most of us never stop to add up all those pennies. What it comes down to is that in your head you are either a 'coupon person' or you're not. If you are, congratulations. If you're not, what happens is that you've trained your eyes never to notice coupons, and you haven't got over your mental resistance to cutting the things out, keeping them in your wallet or purse, and taking them with you when you go shopping.

Well, if you want to spend less, this is about as pain-free as it gets. These savings are already being handed to you for nothing. You don't have to make any sacrifices, any compromises, you don't have to go without anything. All you have to do is make the mental shift to being a 'coupon person'.

Milk your

loyalty

My wife hates supermarket loyalty cards. She reckons it's like Big Brother spying on you, knowing everything you buy. She does actually use them, but every so often she does a weekly shop and doesn't hand over her card so they don't know it's her. It gives her a feeling of satisfaction that she's got one over on them.

Personally I think she's a trifle paranoid (in the nicest possible way), given the savings they can earn you. The fact is that the card is free and the vouchers and offers come without strings attached – except from my wife's point of view, since you do have to use the card to get the benefits.

Not only can you use all the vouchers and offers that go with the card, but with some card schemes you can also collect points from other retailers. And the websites that go with the cards also have additional offers, so check them out. I know people who deliberately shop at a variety of supermarkets in order to get the pick of the offers.

The only thing to remember here is that a half-price deal on something you wouldn't otherwise buy is *not* a saving. It's an extra cost.

MAKE THE MOST OF
SUPERMARKETS

The big supermarkets are all desperate to do whatever they can to get and keep your business. They assume – rightly in most cases – that cost is a big deal to you. So they're always finding new ways to save you money.

Broadly speaking, the best approach to shopping is to take a list of what you need to buy and stick to it. However, that doesn't mean you can't look for the best offer on an item on the list. Just because you normally buy branded cornflakes, for example, don't be blind to an offer on own-brand cornflakes. Just because you were planning spaghetti for this evening's meal doesn't mean you can't switch to another form of pasta if it's on a two-for-one deal.

If you look out for the best deals, you'll find the supermarket displays them pretty prominently. There are BOGOFs (buy one get one free), two-for-ones and three-for-twos, reduced prices for a fixed period, and items that come with useful vouchers and coupons.

I know many people who just never think to look for these deals, and plenty of others who save several pounds a week by really making the most of supermarket shopping.

Just make sure, if you go for a three-for-two or whatever, that you will definitely use all three before any use-by date. It's *not* a saving if you pay for two, get three but use only one.

Shop for quality, not quantity

I once wanted to give my then girlfriend (now my wife) a special breakfast in bed. So I nipped up the road to the florist to buy a single red rose to put on the breakfast tray. The florist asked, 'Wouldn't you like a bouquet of a dozen red roses?' To which I replied, 'No, one will work.' For some reason, when I relayed this to my wife, she seemed to think that I wasn't entering into the spirit of the thing (but I was right).

Why waste money unnecessarily? Why not buy one fantastic firework instead of a dozen cheap ones? You'll get a better result at a better price. Or liven up your existing party clothes with a fantastic new belt or piece of jewellery instead of buying a whole new outfit.

You can spend less this way on your Christmas shopping, clothes shopping, even food shopping – a basic recipe can be made really impressive with just one fancy ingredient, rather than feeling you have to splash out on trendy food. Something ordinary can be lifted into the exotic with cep mushrooms, or truffle oil, or dragon fruit. And if you enjoy the occasional bottle of wine, why not have one glass of something really good instead of a whole bottle of plonk?

Shop for quality, not for price

Now you're going for quality goods, you'll find there's another benefit. Really good quality stuff lasts longer than cheap rubbish, so stop buying any bargain you can lay your hands on just because it's cheap. Nope, that's a false economy. And I should know – I used to do it all the time. I'm too impatient by far – if I wanted something I wanted it now, and if I couldn't afford it, I'd buy a cheaper, shoddier version.

That's where I went wrong. Because the cheap version wore out, broke down, fell apart, sooner than the decent one would have done. Look, I'm not suggesting you live beyond your means. That would just be silly in a book about how to spend less. What I'm saying is that if you can't afford what you want, you should go without. Save up until you can afford it. Otherwise you'll be saddled with some piece of rubbish that doesn't really do the job.

I have three young children. When it comes to buying them clothes, decent quality stuff will last and be passed down through all three. Whereas if I buy the cheapest clothes I can get for the oldest, I'm lucky if they last until he's outgrown them, let alone passed them on to his siblings. So (quick bit of mental arithmetic here), so long as the clothes I buy cost no more than three times the cheapest ones, I'm quids in if I shop for quality, not price.

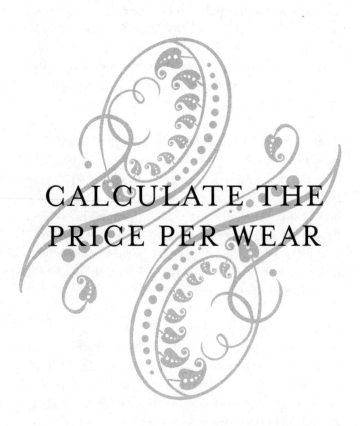

CALCULATE THE
PRICE PER WEAR

I s it worth spending £150 on a coat? Or £60 on a pair of boots? Well, that depends on how much use you're going to get out of them. So why not do as a good friend of mine does and calculate the 'price per wear'. If you're buying a fancy coat to wear to a wedding and may wear it only twice this year, it will be costing you £75 each time you wear it (using the price example above). If you're going to wear it five times a week for the colder half of the year, it's costing you more like £1.15 each time.

This is a really clever way of getting you to focus on the amount of use you'll get from the thing, and then assess its real value. £75 a day seems a lot to spend on a coat when times are tight, whereas £1.15 seems far more reasonable (assuming you have £150 in the first place, of course).

My friend uses this primarily for clothes shopping. But in fact, of course, you can apply it to all sorts of things, from kitchen gadgets to children's toys. Once you can see what value you're getting from the thing, it makes it far easier to turn down a foolhardy purchase.

DECIDE
WHAT IT'S
WORTH

Here's another clothes shopping strategy that you can extend to other products as well. What you have to do is resist looking at the price until you've tried the thing on and looked in the mirror. If you like it, you then decide how much you're prepared to spend on it. You can use the 'price per wear' calculation above to help you make this decision.

Of course, now what you do is take it off and look at the price. If it's more than you fixed on, you don't buy it. Yes, I know that's the difficult bit, and making yourself walk away can be hard. You may be tempted to rethink your notional price up to the actual price. But if you're serious about spending less, you can't do that.

Tell you what, I'll make it a bit easier for you. Don't tell yourself you're never going to buy it. Tell yourself you'll wait until the sales and see if the price comes down to your level. You'll feel so smug when it does that it'll be worth the wait. And if it doesn't … well, then you've saved even more money and you know that the thing wasn't worth that much to you.

BE MAIL
ORDER
SAVVY

Shopping by mail order makes a lot of sense, especially if you live in the sticks. Even in the middle of a big city, though, it's still worthwhile. The carriage charges are often lower than the travel or petrol costs of going to the shops, and it saves time too, which, as we saw earlier, helps to save you money.

If you really want to spend less, however, you can get more than this out of mail order. There are lots of offers available if you look out for them, such as:

- *Pick the companies that offer* free returns.
- *See if postage is free* above a certain amount, and wait until you've got a big enough order.
- *Some companies give you a discount* for ordering online.
- *You can sometimes save delivery charges* by collecting the item from your local store and still claim the online ordering discount.
- *You can often get things cheaper* if you wait for the sales.
- *Supermarkets offer lower delivery charges* for certain slots in the day or week.
- *Many online order systems offer you a discount* if you enter a voucher code. If you search on Google, you can often find codes. Enter the name of the store plus the word 'voucher' or 'coupon'.

Check out the benefit of brands

Sometimes it's worth paying extra for a good brand – you'll get a better product that will last longer, perform better or whatever. Then again, you might just be wasting your money. For example, you can pay anything from under a tenner up to £100 for a stick of mascara, but is it worth it?

Well, the answer is that it depends on the product. Some expensive products really do make a big difference, while others are simply charging you for the name. So which is which? You need to do your research.

In the case of make-up, I can tell you. No, this isn't from personal experience – I haven't myself tried out all the products. But I have done my research, and I have discovered where you do and don't need to splash out if you want the best. When it comes to make-up, the things you might as well buy cheap include concealer, lipstick and mascara. Meanwhile there really is superior technology in the more expensive foundations and lip glosses, so if it matters to you, you can justify buying these. When it comes to shampoo and conditioner, there just isn't any point in spending a lot of money, and the same goes for face masks, hand creams and so on.

If you're planning to buy a car, or a children's toy, or a joint of meat, or a shoulder bag, just do your research. Check it out online or ask someone whose opinion on the subject you trust, and find out what you're actually getting for the extra money other than the name.

ASK YOURSELF IF
YOU NEED IT

It's easy to get sucked into buying things that you don't even need at all. Look around your house. I'll bet it's full of things you never even use. I know mine is. I'm not just talking about the drawer full of plastic bags waiting to be reused, which is filling up faster than anyone can use up plastic bags. I'm talking about gadgets, and objects, and ornaments you don't actually like much, and jars of bizarre food in the cupboard which are well past their use-by date.[1]

Do you know, you don't actually need a thing to take the cores out of apples – a knife does the job perfectly well. Nor do you need fabric conditioner, at least not for 99 per cent of your wash. Nor cleanser, toner and moisturiser (most men manage fine without all this stuff); if you really want to avoid wrinkles, don't smoke or drink and stay out of the sun.[2]

When money is tight, why not question everything you buy to make sure it really is going to earn its keep? If not, don't give it house-room.

[1] There must be a recipe *somewhere* that calls for miniature figs marinated in wine. But it's too late now.
[2] And even then I bet you still get them eventually.

ALWAYS TRY
TO BUY IN
BULK

Whether it's five-litre containers of shampoo or washing-up liquid, or buying everything you need at once from a single supplier so you can ask for a discount, it pays to buy in bulk.

If you buy your shampoo and the like in large quantities, you don't have to keep a gigantic container in the bathroom. Keep it in the garage or cellar, or under the kitchen sink and decant it into smaller containers to use. You can even buy cheap (but serviceable) products and pour them carefully into bottles labelled for expensive products, if that appeals to your sense of humour.

This is great for household products, bathroom stuff and baby stuff, among other things. Cash and carrys are great, but you can bulk buy online too. I have one friend who swears by it and tells me that he emails online retailers who sell all the products he wants and makes them an offer – 'I've got an order here for £400. I can either cut it down, or shop around, or you can give me a good discount and I'll buy the lot from you now.' Many online companies will offer between 10 and 20 per cent discount when presented with that choice.

Try smaller

companies

for size

Following on from the last tip, you're far more likely to haggle successfully with smaller companies. In fact, they're generally more flexible and much more likely to give you useful extras or a better deal. Whether it's online retailers or independent local shops or market stalls, you'll generally get a better deal from the smaller sellers.

You'll also find that being a regular customer will bring you all sorts of money-saving benefits, from discounts to free samples. Just as local butchers used to keep sausages under the counter during wartime rationing for their best customers, nowadays smaller retailers who rely on your business want to make sure they keep it. So be loyal to your best suppliers, and make sure they know it. They may be struggling too, and will do whatever it takes to keep hold of their best customers.

GET INTO
THE HAGGLING
HABIT

There's not much point in asking the checkout assistant in Tesco's if they'll knock 10p off the baked beans. But there are plenty of places you can successfully haggle. It's just a matter of getting over that British reserve that thinks it's rude to haggle – unless you're in a foreign country, of course, when it's obligatory. (Or, for some reason, when buying a used car.)

Well, you could do all your shopping in Mediterranean bazaars or Arab souks. Then again, it would be a whole lot easier just to get into the habit of haggling here. Here are a few tips to get you started:

- *First, don't think of it as haggling* – think of it as asking for a discount. That should feel less embarrassing.

- *Pick your retailer.* The big chain stores aren't going to take kindly to this approach, and in any case, you'll be dealing with an employee who doesn't have the authority to agree to it, even if they admire your front. Ideally you want to be talking to the owner, or at least someone senior.

- *Ask if there's a discount available.* Rehearse saying, 'I'd really like this but it's £10 more than I'd budgeted.'

- *If they won't give a discount* – or you don't want to ask – see if they'll throw something extra in as well.

- *Practise haggling with online retailers,* as you can do it by email – far less embarrassing if you're feeling very British about the whole thing. Once you start getting results you can get braver about trying it with face-to-face retailers too.

Never pay the asking price

This isn't just about haggling. It's about not paying the first price you see for something. There's really no excuse for it these days, with so many easily accessible prices from online sellers, price comparison websites, eBay and marketplace options, asking for discounts and so on.

Make yourself a promise that you'll never buy any one-off item, or anything for over, say, £10, without getting at least three prices for it first. Don't forget to check delivery costs and so on to make sure you're establishing the full cost before you buy.

I know a chap who does this routinely, and often tells me with great glee about the latest bargain he's picked up. He sometimes buys items from overseas which still work out cheaper even with the delivery charges. It can be hugely satisfying to know you've got the best deal you possibly could.

Buy with selling in mind

Sometimes in life you want the best, but you don't necessarily want it for the lifetime of the thing. Maybe it's a car, or some kind of baby equipment, or some fancy electronic equipment (not that you're wasting money on gadgets, of course, but maybe you need it for work).

The smart thing to do here is to buy, having psychologically committed to selling the item on when you've finished with it. And the even smarter thing to do is to take that into account when you buy it. So check out the resale value of the things you're considering (eBay is the most obvious way), and buy the products you can sell on for the smallest loss. Often these are better items than you would otherwise want to pay for. It's amazing how much certain desirable items will fetch second hand – sometimes even within a whisker of the full retail price (especially if people get carried away bidding for things in online auctions). It pays to do your research.

This isn't going to work unless you commit yourself to selling on when you've finished with the thing. And that means looking after it while you've got it. Think of it as being on loan. In the long term, though, you'll find you can end up with better quality products at a lower cost to you. In other words, it's win/win.

NET YOURSELF A BARGAIN

The Internet is a wonderful thing, whether you're buying or selling. It gives you access to so many potential buyers if you have something to sell, and to so many sellers if you're looking to buy.

One of the best ways to spend less is to familiarise yourself with sites like eBay, where individuals just like you and me can sell things they no longer want – or buy things someone else no longer wants. It's simple to register, there are plenty of safety mechanisms in place, paying is easy – go and check it out if you aren't already using it.

eBay is great for buying and selling almost anything, and the most enthusiastic users I've encountered are those who use it for kids' clothes. Many grown-ups, unless we're appallingly cash-happy buyers, wear our clothes until they're worn out.[1] At least if we're on an economy drive we have that option. But kids outgrow theirs, and those things they wear only once a week – ballet shoes, leotards, ski clothes, football boots – are the perfect items to buy and sell on eBay and similar websites.

If you haven't discovered freecycle.org yet, that's another site to check out. Anyone with something to get rid of just offers it free to other members. Usually the buyer collects – the website will direct you to your local branch. I've known people pick up free Christmas presents for their kids, rabbit hutches, lawnmowers, fridges – you name it. It's one of the best ways I know to cut down your spending.

Well, these are just a couple of popular examples. But get friendly with your PC and you'll find a host of websites to help you buy and sell more cost-effectively – and even get what you want for nothing.

---

[1] Or unless we very suddenly lose or gain weight, of course.

SHOP
TWICE

If you decide you can afford to go out shopping for clothes or Christmas presents or things for the house, set aside a couple of shopping sessions. The first one is for looking only – make a note of what you like and where, so you can go back for it later.

The second trip is not for looking, it's just for going back to pick up the things you earmarked first time. You should find that when it comes to it, you can resist a lot of the things you'd been tempted by, and only go back for a couple of things you really want. It's a form of built-in cooling-off period, if you like. Sometimes the effort of going back to collect the thing can be enough to put you off – which is a sure sign that you didn't really want it.

Join
mailing
lists

If you shop online – and you would if, like me, you lived miles from the nearest shops – it's always worth signing up for the email newsletters and mailing lists of the companies you use.

Why would you want to do that, you may be wondering. You already get more spam than you can cope with in your inbox, without adding loads of solicited stuff you don't need. Aha! That's where you're wrong. You see, almost all Internet retailers send out special offers to their customers all year round. So your inbox will be buzzing with emails offering 'free delivery this month' or '10% off orders over £50'.

Think about it. If your local greengrocer, or newsagent, or baker has to work hard to keep you loyal, how much harder is it for online retailers – who have never even met you – to get you to keep coming back? So they tempt you with plenty of offers and bargains and discounts and deals.

Of course, you have to be disciplined about this. It's no good taking up every offer that comes your way, or you'll be skint amidst a pile of stuff you just don't need. That would be silly. But if you make it a rule to buy only those products you've already identified as being worthwhile, things you're maybe already buying from these sellers, this is a great way to save money.

BUY AT
AUCTION

I know, it's that scary worry that you'll develop a nervous tic and find you've bought a priceless artwork for millions,[1] when all you wanted was a box of assorted second-hand crockery for a fiver. But it's worth getting over the nerves because you can save a lot of money at auction, especially for bigger items such as cars, computers, electrical goods, houses and land.

The crucial thing is to set your maximum price in advance and then not to go above it. You need to be absolutely clear about how much the thing is worth to you, and set your level accordingly. And of course you need to have done your research thoroughly – checking out both the item and the market value. Of course, you know that you must be very disciplined, clearly identify what you want first, and if you don't get it at your pre-decided price be ready to walk – not buy something else to fill the disappointment void.

If you really don't trust yourself not to get carried away, the foolproof way round this is to get someone else to go along and bid on your behalf, having told them what price they're not to exceed. I say foolproof – obviously if you ask an excitable and impulsive optimist to do this for you you may get what you deserve. But ask someone careful and level-headed and you'll be entirely safe.

---

[1] I've never understood how something priceless can have a price.

GET
COMPETITIVE

I know one woman, who is a dedicated competition enterer, who decided to win as much of the cost of her wedding as she could. Simply by entering competitions she got all the drink for her wedding paid for, plus a relaxing meal for four cooked in her own house by a professional chef the week before the big day, plus a luxury fortnight's honeymoon in an exotic location. A year later she won herself a three- month round-the-world trip.

So, you see, it really is worth entering competitions. She tells me that a lot of people are put off on the assumption that they don't stand a chance against all the other entrants, but actually many competitions have far fewer entrants than you'd expect. You can sometimes take the prize in cash (and even if you can't you can still flog it if you don't want it), and winnings are tax free.

There are techniques and strategies for winning, especially where slogans and tie-breakers are concerned, such as making them rhyme or including a pun. Have a search online (try 'competitions' for starters) and you'll find websites specifically aimed at passing on tips for winning competitions.

KNOW WHEN TO SELL ... AND WHEN TO BUY

Whether you're buying in the shops, selling on eBay or going to auction, it pays to get the timing right. Generally this is pretty obvious, but you do need to plan ahead. For example, evening dresses are most in demand in the run-up to Christmas, and then go on sale in January. So whether you're going to the sales or dealing online, you want to buy in January and sell in November or December. Clearly that means that if you want to buy a dress to wear to all your exciting and glamorous Christmas parties, you need to be thinking about it 11 months in advance. If it's a wedding dress you want, they'll be sold off at the end of the summer – summer being the peak time for weddings.

If you want to buy a second-hand barbecue, or an open-top sports car, or a boat, prices will hit the bottom in late autumn and start to pick up again in the spring. Christmas decorations are cheap in January and peak from September onwards. Buy a swimsuit in November, and sell your winter coat in October.

I'm sure you can work it out for yourself from here. Just remember that prices aren't constant throughout the year, and you can spend a lot less money if you're canny about when you buy and when you sell. Yes, you do have to learn to think ahead and be very organised, but boy, can it be worth it.

Support

your local

farmer

Have you ever visited your local farmers' market? If not, I highly recommend it. It's a fun way to spend a couple of hours (except possibly if you have small children) and you can often pick up a free snack from all the samples on offer of everything from fruit to cheese, meat, wine and more.

The food at farmers' markets isn't universally cheap, though it's generally good value. However, you'll find that organic food tends to be cheaper than the supermarket equivalent. And the quality is almost always superb.

The best way to save money at these markets, however, is to get there about an hour before closing time. Lots of stallholders will have food they need to offload, and if you're prepared to haggle (and even if you're not) you can pick up some great bargains.

STICK TO
TAP WATER

Do you have any idea how much you spend on bottled water? Work it out – go on. OK, I'll give you a clue. If you drink one litre a day, it's costing you around £260 a year, depending on the brand, obviously. And if you drink more than that, you can do the calculations yourself. Likewise if you buy it in cafés or restaurants it will be costing you far more. In fact, bottled water in the UK costs about as much as petrol.[1]

And that's before you start considering the impact on the environment of bottled water in almost every way – production, packaging and transport.

Now think what you could be doing with that money instead. You could feed your family for an extra fortnight or more, go out for the evening several times, do a good chunk of your Christmas shopping, buy your mum flowers every month … oh, all sorts of things, even if they're just boring but important things like being able to pay the bills. You could even buy yourself a water filter if you really don't like the idea of drinking water straight from the tap, and a reusable bottle to take it with you everywhere.

And if you're thinking, 'Ah, but I can't get fizzy water out of the tap, can I?' you'd be right. But you can buy a water carbonator and still have change from all the money you'll save.

[1] And you wouldn't drink that, would you?

CHANGE
YOUR
HABITS

H ave you ever stopped to think about all the expensive food habits you've got into? OK, you're going to be drinking tap water from now on, but that's not the only habit most of us need to change. Here are a few more ideas, and if they don't apply to you, clock what you eat or drink each day and see where you're spending more than you need:

- *Loads of us drink a glass or two of wine* at home of an evening (red for me please). Even if you're steering clear of the Château Margaux, a couple of bottles a week is still costing you a tenner. Most of the people I know who crack this habit say they feel much better, as well as richer, for it.

- *If you commute, do you stop by a coffee stall or takeaway* for a double espresso to wake you up, or a skinny mocha latte spressochino thingy? Or even just a cup of tea? If so, would you like to pause now to multiply the cost of that by five to see what you're spending each week? And now multiply that by 48 for your annual morning coffee expenditure? Maybe you'd be better off taking a flask to work, or a bottle of (tap) water.

- *Do you pop out at lunchtime to buy lunch?* What does that cost you over a year? You could make up luxury sandwiches at home with great ingredients and still save money.

Buy less food

Right, I'm going to bang on about food for a bit now. And if you want to know why – well, it's because we spend a very significant amount of our income on food (often without realising it), and it's the easiest and most painless place to make instant savings and develop new habits that will save us money without thinking in the future. So let's get cooking …

Do you know how much food we throw away each year? A quarter of all we buy. Yes, really. Of course, some of that is made up of banana skins and used teabags, which I'm not suggesting you eat, but the vast majority of it is perfectly good food that we just haven't eaten. So if we could buy only what we were going to eat, we'd save a quarter of our food bill – that's at least several hundred pounds a year.

So how are we going to do that, then? OK, here are a few things to get you started ...

- *Plan what you're going to eat before you shop.* And don't buy anything unless you know when you're going to eat it. No thinking 'Those pears look nice' unless you put back some of the apples you just selected. Your fruit consumption won't go up because you've bought pears, so you'll end up leaving the apples to go brown and mouldy.

- *Make sure you know how food should be stored best.* Otherwise you'll throw away food you wanted to eat but that has gone off. If you aren't going to get to it before it's too late, put it in the freezer to extend its life.

- *A 'use by' date tells you for how long the food will be safe to eat.* But a 'best before' date is only for advice, on foods that won't do you serious harm if eaten past their best (except for eggs, apparently). You can ignore 'best before' labels and use your own judgement as to whether the food is still OK.

BUY CHEAPER
FOOD

What is it that stops so many of us buying own brands? Is it just plain snobbery, or do we really think there's something wrong with them? Actually, a lot of top-brand manufacturers repackage exactly the same products as own brands for the big supermarket chains. When you buy them you might in fact be buying top-brand digestive biscuits in a different wrapper, or leading baby wipes under a different name.

So one of the most obvious ways to spend less is to switch to own brands. Try them with an open mind. If you really hate them, you can decide whether it's worth paying the extra for a brand you like – it's your choice. I'm only making suggestions here – it's your money.

And have you ever stopped to see how much more you're paying for, say, pre-washed, trimmed and packaged runner beans than for loose beans that need a bit of a clean? Or potatoes? Or carrots, or onions, or parsnips, or lettuces, or apples? Most fruit and vegetables come in lots of different prices according to variety, packaging, preparation, cleaning and so on.

You may well be surprised to find that you can carry on buying the same basic foods in the same supermarket and cut loads off your regular shopping bill, just by switching the brand or variety. Go on – and then you can hold a blind tasting for your family and see if they can even tell the difference.

Be a sneaky cheapskate

I know what you're going to say. Your partner won't eat it if it's not Heinz. The kids won't touch it if it isn't Kellogg's. The dog will only eat Winalot. Well, there's a way round that one.

If you think the kids won't eat own-brand cornflakes, decant the packet into the old Kellogg's packet when it's empty, and see if they even notice. I'd be surprised if they do. Don't tell your partner you're opening a can of baked beans that isn't made by Heinz. Wash out old jars and bottles and pour the new ketchup and mayonnaise into them.

You can decide whether you want to keep this up indefinitely, or whether to tell them once they've eaten the new version without complaining. Personally I wouldn't be able to resist the smug glow of telling them I'd got one up on them.

Now the only excuse for not buying cheaper products is if *you* won't eat them …

Cook for yourself

It's easy to get into the habit of buying pre-packed food and ready-meals. At the end of a long day, who wants to cook? Well, someone who's skint, for a start. Look, this is just one of those habit things again. We all say we're tired and don't have time to cook, but that's actually just an excuse. There are plenty of quick and easy meals you can cook for yourself that are nutritious, and not packed with all the salt and additives that most ready-meals are. If you don't believe me, here are a few suggestions:

- *cheese on toast* topped with tomatoes
- *quick-cook spaghetti* with spinach leaves and walnuts stirred in
- *herb omelette*
- *quick-cook rice* with frozen peas, tinned sweetcorn and mushrooms.

Right, that's enough. You can think of the rest for yourself. Even if you start off resolving to cook for yourself just once or twice a week, it'll save you money, and you can build up from there.

Of course, once you've got into the habit of cooking for yourself, you can also cook extra for the freezer. That means you will have days when you get home from work late and tired, and you *can* have a ready-meal – one you prepared yourself.

USE YOUR LEFTOVERS

Now here's a suggestion your grandmother would approve of. I know it sounds obvious, but most of us don't do it these days. Of course, if you've planned your shopping well and bought less food, this will be less of a challenge. But there are still times when food will get left over, and you don't want to be paying for another meal when you have the makings of a perfectly good one already.

For a start, you can plan your leftovers into your shopping. You know perfectly well what will get left over from certain meals because you've cooked them so often. Sunday roasts, the kids' favourites and so on. If you know you're going to have potatoes and veg left over, plan to cook bubble and squeak for the next meal. Then all you need to buy are some sausages or something to go with it. Much better than cooking another meal and then opening the fridge and saying pathetically, 'Oh dear. Whatever shall I do with all these leftover vegetables?'

Even if you don't know what will be left over, you can still plan for every third or fourth meal to be made up on the spot from leftovers and food fast approaching its 'use by' date. That will save the cost of another meal. Then get creative about using up whatever is there. Make casseroles, and risottos, and curries, and pasta bakes, and salads.

If you're really worried there won't be any leftovers (when did that last happen after three or four meals?), just make sure there's something in the cupboard you can use as a fallback such as a tin of beans, so no one has to starve.

For more ideas visit www.lovefoodhatewaste.com for masses of tips on using up leftovers, from pesto to fromage frais.

USE YOUR FREEZER

The point about the freezer is that you can avoid throwing away food by freezing it before it's gone off. Yes, indeed, you can cook extra quantities of meals for the freezer too, but that will save you time rather than money – apart from the saving of cooking for yourself. But where the freezer really comes into its own as a money-saving device is in extending the life of your leftovers. It also gives you a great feeling of satisfaction to have a well-stocked freezer full of healthy inexpensive meals, instead of overpackaged additive-full shop-bought stuff.

Sometimes you have unopened packets of sausages or something that are obviously ripe for freezing,[1] but here are a few less obvious ways of getting mileage from your freezer:

- *Turn stale bread into* croutons or breadcrumbs and freeze them.

- *Freeze lemon or orange juice* in ice trays to use in cooking later.

- *Freeze portions of leftover sauces* such as pesto, horseradish, mint sauce and so on – all those things that say 'refrigerate and eat within six weeks' on the jar.

- *Use leftover cheese* to make cheese sauce and freeze it – you can throw in any cheese you've got, from cream cheese to fromage frais, stilton to goat's cheese.

- *Freeze chopped fresh herbs* (which you can buy only in absurdly large bunches) in water in ice trays to add to soups, stews and curries. Or mix herbs or garlic with butter and freeze in small quantities for garlic or herb bread, or to toss vegetables in before serving.

Once you've got into the right mindset, I'm sure you'll come up with a hundred clever tricks I haven't thought of. Just look at those leftovers and calculate what they cost you, and that should spur you into getting value from your freezer.

[1] If sausages can be ripe.

COOK LESS FOOD

B oy, am I rubbish at this. I'm too used to cooking for a large family. But just because you're getting clever with using up your leftovers, that doesn't mean you shouldn't still try to reduce them. After all, if you buy only what you're going to eat, that's the most cost-effective approach of all.

Carbohydrates are among the most commonly discarded foods. They may not be the most expensive, but they still cost money (oh no, I'm sounding like my mother). So freeze half a loaf of bread until you've eaten the other half, and don't cook too much rice or too many potatoes.

Most of us have favourite dishes we cook regularly. So make a conscious effort to notice how much of them your family actually eats. You can do this in terms of raw ingredients – I've learnt that my young children love mashed potato and will eat the equivalent of one raw potato each. Cook any more than that, and I'll end up with leftovers.

Another option is to gauge it by the dish you cook it in. I have one oval dish that I know is just the right size to feed my family if I use it for macaroni cheese, or lasagne, or moussaka, or a pie.[1]

As a useful rule of thumb, by the way, a (healthy) portion of fruit or vegetables is roughly the size of your fist. Here's another one: a coffee mug of rice will serve four adults.

[1] So why, in heaven's name, do I always cook more than will fit in it?

Eat on the cheap

When times are tight, the answer is not to eat less (although for some of us it wouldn't do much harm) but to eat cheaper food. And the trick is to build up a repertoire of foods that are tasty, healthy, filling and affordable.

Your best bet is to come up with meals that are based on filling carbohydrates, as these are generally cheap foods. This book is about spending less, not about being healthy, but obviously it'll be better for you to eat brown rice, wholewheat pasta, semi-skimmed milk and so on. I'll leave that to you.

On this principle, good cheap meals include risottos, pasta dishes, root vegetable soups (served with bread), cauliflower cheese (or most things in cheese sauce really), bean dishes and so on. If you're economising on these main meals, you will probably be able to afford a few tasty treats to go with them as an added bonus.

When it comes to meat, learn how to get the best out of the cheaper cuts. If you're stewing or braising rather than roasting, frying or grilling, most of the cheaper cuts are at their best. And when tenderness is no longer a problem because you're cooking it slow and moist, they're often the most flavoursome of all. Plus it can be great fun weirding out your kids by dishing up offal, much of which is actually very tasty.

BECOME A
VEGETARIAN

All right, so not everyone wants to give up their Sunday roast, or their steak, or their favourite chicken casserole. But the fact is that meat is one of the most expensive ingredients we routinely cook with, and the simplest way to cut your weekly shopping bill is usually just to eliminate the meat. And if you can't face that, why not just reduce it? You could eat a meat-based meal just three or four times a week.

One of the biggest problems for many meat-eaters is that we're so used to cooking meat and two veg that we wouldn't have a clue what to cook if we became part-time vegetarians. You can't live on nut roast three times a week, surely?

Look, vegetarians are people just like us, and if they can manage to feed themselves it must be possible. Granted, if you're not a keen cook it can seem like a lot of hard work. So why not start with vegetarian versions of things you already cook? Casseroles without the meat (oh, all right then, just a bit of bacon to add flavour), or vegetarian versions of lasagne, or moussaka, or bolognese sauce.

Back in the days when I was well and truly skint, I used to cook a vegetarian bolognese sauce for my teenage kids. I'd just throw together whatever vegetables were around and cook them as I would mincemeat, with tinned tomatoes and so on. Then I put the whole lot through the blender – it comes out the consistency and flavour of a bolognese sauce. I used to take particular delight in including mushrooms because one of my sons claimed to be allergic to them, but couldn't tell they were there.

Grow your own

W ell, here's an obvious way to save a bit of cash. The problem is that you don't have the time, the space, the energy, the tools, the expertise. But apart from that, you're rocking.

Listen, growing your own doesn't *have* to mean creating a huge dedicated vegetable patch and spending every Sunday lovingly tending it and nurturing your prize-winning turnips to the peak of perfection. If you think that's what you're in for, I'm not surprised you don't fancy it.

But you can start smaller than you think, and expand only if and when you want to. Even if you simply grew your favourite herbs on the kitchen windowsill in the summer – say basil, parsley and lemon thyme – you'd be saving on buying them to flavour your food (or going without). That alone would be worth it. Even if all you have is a windowsill, you could grow strawberries in a window box alongside the herbs.

If you have a patio or paved area there are growbags (and it's amazing what you can do with a few growbags). Or containers to hold strawberries or fruiting shrubs like blueberries. With a small patch of garden you can grow a few lettuces in among your flowers, and some herbs and maybe garlic or radishes. And when that's going well you can start to think bigger. When I first started to grow vegetables I assumed that as I didn't know what I was doing they'd all come up withered and full of holes, if they even came up at all. But to my surprise, I followed the instructions on the packet and almost all of them grew strong and healthy and were really tasty. Try it.

And if you want to tell me that you don't even have a windowsill because you live underground – well, you have the perfect conditions to grow your own mushrooms.

Free food

I f you live anywhere near open ground or countryside, or ever drive through it, there is food you can find at the right times of year that will save you money in the shops. The most obvious of these, for good reason, are blackberries.

You might be thinking, 'Does he think I'm daft? That doesn't save me money – I'm not going to be buying blackberries when times are hard – not at supermarket prices.' Ha! But sooner or later you'd have had to buy something else instead to dish up, when you could be eating blackberry and apple pie.

Now, I'm not pretending you can realistically scavenge all the food you need, but every little helps and there's delicious food to be had for free. As well as blackberries in late summer and early autumn, how about nettle soup with the young spring shoots? No, I'm not a card-carrying hippy (OK, I was once, but that was a long time ago), but if you enjoy spinach soup[1] you'll enjoy this too. Just wear gloves until you've got the nettles into the pan.

Then there are elderberries, bilberries/blueberries, wild garlic leaves, sorrel, sloes (make your own sloe gin) … and if you live by the sea all sorts of seaweeds and samphire. Go and get Richard Mabey's book *Food for Free* out of the library and see what you're missing. You might even be brave enough to try the edible mushrooms and other fungi (if you are very sure you know edible from the rest – best to make sure). There's so much pleasure to be had getting food from the wild. An adventure day out and free food into the bargain – got to be worth it.

And I haven't even mentioned fishing …

[1] Actually I hate it, but I'm told lots of people love it – maybe you're one of them.

STAY IN

I t may be stating the obvious, but loads of us don't really think about it consciously. When you opt for a night in instead of a night out, you save money not only on the evening's entertainment, but quite possibly also on transport, babysitting, dry cleaning your party gear and all the rest of it. Yes, I hear you cry, but that's not 'without being miserable'? Where's the fun in that?

Well, of course you don't have to stay in on your own, moping about your lack of social life. You could invite friends round and get hammered on home brew for a quarter of the price of going out and doing it. This is the student approach, as you'll know if you've been a student. Of course, you won't want to get hammered on home brew (will you?) but there are all sorts of other ways to have fun with friends at home, from cooking a meal to getting together to watch the final of your favourite reality TV show.

If you socialise a lot, even replacing one night out a week with an evening at home with friends will save you a lot of money and shouldn't cost you any fun at all. And if you take it in turns to be host, then you actually stay at home only one night out of several – the rest you'll be round their houses instead, which still counts as going out or at least as a change of scenery.

GO OUT
LATER

Oooh, this is so blissfully simple. You know when you go out with your mates for an evening, maybe to the pub or out for a drink somewhere? Over the course of an evening you can spend quite a bit of money. More than you probably meant to.

The idea here is that you go out later in the evening. Maybe at 9.30 instead of 8 o'clock. You won't have so much time to spend your money, so you'll spend less. You can still meet up at 8 o'clock if you want to, maybe at someone's house before going out, so you'll still have as much time with your friends. This is great because you still get your evening out, still get to have fun, but find when you get home that there's more cash left in your pocket.

Incidentally, another trick for evenings out with a regular group of friends is to save money on taxi fares home. Just take it in turns to stay sober and drive everyone home. It's not so bad to stick to soft drinks, and it's cheaper of course, and your turn only comes round every few times you go out.

HOLD
A SWAP
SHOP

Chances are that you're not the only person you know without money to burn. So here's an idea that will save you and your friends money. Invite a few friends over and ask everyone to bring along three things they don't want. Then all you do is swap until everyone has three new items that have cost them nothing.

You can theme the evening if you want to so everyone brings along kids' toys, or clothes, kitchen equipment,[1] Christmas gifts or gardening stuff – whatever you're all into.

If you're smart you'll have noticed that this is a great way to have a fun social evening on the cheap too. You can add to the general aim of the evening by each bringing along something to eat as well, so no one has to spend too much on food.

[1] Why are the backs of everyone's kitchen cupboards cluttered with gadgets they never use?

Bargain
competition

If you enjoy going out shopping with friends, the problem can be that you egg each other on to buy things you can't really afford. It's so tricky when your mate is saying, 'Oh that's great! You've got to get it!' to keep a clear head and resist temptation. If you're a bloke thinking this is a really girly clothes-shopping thing, well, it's not. At least, not exclusively. I've seen blokes do exactly the same thing buying second-hand cars, or going round the boat jumble.

What you need to do is find a friend who operates to roughly the same kind of budget as you. Then you make a pact designed to keep your spending down. For example, you compete to see who can find the best bargain, or the best product for under a fiver, or who can spend the least. You could even have a special award for anyone who manages to get through the whole shopping trip without spending any money at all. You can still enjoy yourself, after all, and make a mental note of what you really want to buy once you've saved up.

SET UP A
BABYSITTING
CIRCLE

Once you have kids, going out means you pay twice – once for the evening's entertainment, and then again for the babysitter. An evening out can cost you a pretty penny.

Well, there are ways to save money on your evening out, as we've seen elsewhere, and there's also a great way to save money on babysitting – even without a friendly set of grandparents nearby.

All you do is find other friends in exactly the same boat as you, and take it in turns to babysit for each other. If they are in couples, one can stay home with their kids while the other one minds yours. And single parents can join in too, by having your kids to stay over with them. Most of us would gladly spend an evening babysitting for the payoff of an evening out without having to pay a babysitter.

MEET FOR LUNCH

Do you realise that many restaurants offer a fixed-price lunch for less than half the price of dinner? That's got to be worth taking advantage of. I know that if you work and have kids, meeting friends for lunch can be tricky, but so long as you don't fall into both categories you should be able to organise it either during the week or at weekends.

I know lunch seems like a briefer meal than dinner but, really, why should it be? You can still dawdle over your meal as you chat, and take your time over coffee – and keep your evenings free.

Of course you can economise by eating at less expensive establishments, and that's a smart move too. But wherever you eat you can still save money by avoiding evening bookings. In fact, meeting friends for breakfast on a lazy Sunday morning is great too (as I recall from the days before I had kids). You can rendezvous at a civilised hour and read the papers over croissants and orange juice, and discuss how much you're saving.

Share and

share alike

I don't know about you, but I usually finish a good meal out feeling overly full, if not bloated. Eating more than you need is pretty pointless during the good times, but when times are hard it's just plain daft. So don't do it.

Why not share a starter or a pudding with your dining companion? If you hate sharing a plate, like me, you can always ask for an extra plate and divvy up the food before you start eating it (also a good move if you don't trust your companion not to exceed their share of the food).

Or, of course, you can just skip a course. Or follow my wife's preference for ordering two starters instead of a starter followed by a main. The advantage of all of these approaches to keeping the cost down is that none of them entails forgoing your favourite thing on the menu (which is always the priciest). You may have to share it, of course, but hey, you're among friends.

And when you get to the end of the meal … why pay for those expensive coffees and even brandies? Why not go home, or to your friend's place, and drink decent coffee and brandy at supermarket prices instead of inflated restaurant ones?

SWAP YOUR
HOUSE

You can save all your accommodation costs on holiday by staying in someone else's house. There is a downside to this, however – they have to go somewhere while you're using their house, and the idea of house-swapping is (you guessed it) that they come and stay at your gaff.

Now I appreciate that there are some people – control freaks, the extremely houseproud, those who haven't cleaned in 10 years – for whom this is not an attractive arrangement. But for lots of us, it's a great way to make friends and holiday on the cheap.

Make friends? But you'll never see them, will you? No, you won't, but the way house-swapping websites and companies work is that you spend a while getting to know your fellow swappers. So by the time the holiday happens, you know them well enough to be comfortable about letting them in your house. Alternatively you can swap privately with someone you already know, of course.

The companies that arrange house swaps have plenty of advice on how to keep it trouble free (lock away your valuables, that sort of thing), and lots of happy swappers have found it a great way to go on holidays they otherwise couldn't afford.

Book late

I f you book your holiday as late as possible, you'll
often get cheap deals. The less picky you are
about where you stay – or even where you
holiday – the greater the potential savings. If you are
dead set on a particular destination, then this doesn't
always work, as flexibility as well as lateness is key to
the big bargains.

Of course, lots of us don't like the feeling of not
knowing where we're going until the last minute,
especially if we're travelling with the family or as a
group. That's understandable. But it doesn't mean
you can't still save money. It's easy to focus on the
cost of flights and perhaps accommodation when
budgeting for your holiday, but there are plenty of
opportunities to spend less on extras such as food,
tourist attractions and pre-flight hotels too. You can
get these through some online holiday companies, or
do a Google search for the name of your destination
or the attraction plus 'coupons' or 'vouchers' and see
what's on offer.

Holiday nearer home

I've travelled a bit in my time. But do you know, the holidays I look back on most fondly have almost all been right here in the UK. Certainly if you have children there is nothing to compare with the beaches of southwest England. All those tropical, white sand, palm-fringed beaches have little to offer but reliable sunbathing. Close your eyes and you might just as well be anywhere – so why pay to be further away than you need to? Cornish beaches, on the other hand – as well as plenty in Wales, Ireland and other parts of the UK – have good sea bathing, great surfing, rock pools to explore, caves, sand, streams to dam. How could you not want to take your kids there?

And if you don't have children with you, I'm absolutely sure there are fascinating places to explore within easy reach of your home. Walking in the hills, boating on the rivers, visiting cultural cities. Beautiful train rides, fascinating historical sites, gourmet restaurants, terrific theatre shows, stunning gardens, exciting theme parks. Get out a map and look at all those places within easy reach that you've never visited. Come on! You're missing so much, and now's the time to go and see it.

Look, I'm not saying you should never go abroad again. I'm just suggesting that when money is tight, it's a great opportunity to do all those things you've never got round to doing closer to home. The holiday glass isn't half empty – it's half full.

For those of us who live in Britain, clearly I can't get away without mentioning the British weather. Of course it's unpredictable; that's its charm. But lots of UK holidays don't rely on the weather. And as my mother used to say whenever it rained on holiday, 'Isn't it wonderful! We've got the beach to ourselves.'

WORK
TO
LIVE

If you can't afford to pay for a holiday, go on a free one. If you earn your keep there are lots of low-cost or even free holidays to be had. Sure, you'll get less free time and less choice of where you go. But for many people that's not the point. If you're doing something you enjoy, and you're meeting new people, you can have a great time. And even if it doesn't turn out to be the best holiday you've ever had – well, it didn't cost you much.

If you're a wildlife and countryside enthusiast there are lots of volunteering holidays to be had. You might be brush-clearing or hedge-laying all day, which isn't for everyone, but it's exactly what some of us enjoy, and you'll learn loads.

There are lots of other ways to holiday while you work. If you decide to do something abroad such as grape-picking or teaching, be aware that you won't get much of a chance to see the place by the time you've done working. However, once you've earned the money, you can stay where you are for a well-earned holiday at the end of your stint.

Avoid

currency

traps

One of the incidental costs of going abroad is buying foreign currency. Not only do you often get stung with an unfavourable rate of exchange, but you'll also get a lower rate when you sell back your currency than you bought it for. So here are a few thoughts on how to spend less on currency:

- *You'll generally get the best exchange rates online.* You certainly won't get them at the airport.
- *Don't buy more than you need.* Even if you get a deal where the buy-back is free of commission, you'll still get a worse rate. You may even be better off paying a commission. The ideal situation is not to have any currency left over. Hard to achieve exactly, but the closer you can get the better.
- *You'll certainly have to pay commission* on traveller's cheques.
- *Taking cash is generally the* cheapest *option, if not necessarily the* safest. However, if you're staying at a hotel with a safe you can keep it in, you should be OK.
- *You can draw cash from ATMs when you're abroad.* Check with your card issuer in advance what they will charge you, both as a transaction fee and as a 'currency loading' fee, so you can work out the most cost-effective way to access foreign currency.

GET THE KIDS
INVOVED

Electricity bills can be a big part of your household expenses. So you need to do what you can to cut down. If you have kids, though, you may well find they scupper you by leaving the lights on, the TV on standby and the computer running all the time. Why should they care? They don't pay the bills.

So motivate them. If there's something in it for them, they're much more likely to make the effort to cut down on electricity use. Try this: if they can help you reduce your regular electricity bill, split a share of the saving with them. That's right – a cash incentive. Obviously there's no point giving them all the savings or you're back where you started. But suppose they save you £10 a month. You could give them 10% of that saving each. That's £1 per child and you should all end up quids in.[1]

Alternatively you can run a competition and give the reward each month to the one who has been best at switching things off. You'll need to be sure you're being fair here, though, or the subsequent row could generate enough heat to power the house on its own. Now there's an idea …

---

[1] Unless you have ten children or more.

THINK HARD
ABOUT
INSURANCE

D o you always take up insurance and warranty offers on stuff like washing machines, or holidays, or pets? Or maybe you never do? Well, not so fast, you need to think this through.

Why do the companies concerned want you to buy their insurance deals? If they were expecting to pay out more than your instalments amount to, they wouldn't offer it, would they? So they must reckon that on average they pay out *less* than you pay in. Well, in that case, the odds are that it will cost you more to buy the insurance than you'd have to pay if the thing broke down. Of course that's a gamble, but the odds are in your favour if you don't buy the cover.

However – not so fast – there is another point to bear in mind. What's the worst-case scenario? If you don't buy the cover, and then you end up unlucky and have to pay for the repairs/replacement/vet bills/missed holiday yourself, could you afford it? Or could you manage without? If your car breakdown could cost you several hundred pounds, maybe you need to pay for the extended warranty just to give you peace of mind, even though you know it'll probably cost you more in the long run. However, if the most your dishwasher is likely to cost you is £150, and you could live without it anyway if you had to, maybe you'd be better off passing on the insurance.

So there isn't a right and a wrong, but the trick is to recognise that the odds are that insurance will cost you more than no insurance, and then think through whether you could cope if the thing broke down.

CHECK
YOUR
STATEMENT

When did you last look at your bank statement in detail? Recently, I hope. How about your standing orders and direct debits? You may find you're paying for things you simply don't need.

For one thing, there may be long-standing regular payments for magazine subscriptions or memberships that just aren't worthwhile at the moment. Do you really still need that copy of *Classic Boat* every month? Are you sure you still want to be a member of Greenpeace?

Then there are things that might be worthwhile in the long term, but perhaps at the moment you could reduce your payments. A private pension, perhaps? Do you have investment schemes that could be put on hold, or even cashed in? Are you running an unnecessary bank account?

So take a good look at everything you're spending, and question it all. Don't bury your head in the sand or it will catch up with you in the end[1] and just make you more miserable. Maybe the answer in many cases is to go on spending it, but don't take any of it for granted.

[1] No, not the sand …

LOOK FOR
THE BEST
DEALS

I nertia. It costs a lot of money. It's so much easier to do nothing than to take action, and about the biggest inertia costs come with household bills.

It really pays to shop around for cheap deals on everything from the digital TV, phone, gas and electricity, through to mortgage, loans and insurance. The fact is that someone else will almost always offer you a better deal than your current one, just to get your business.

So get over the inertia – that's the trickiest bit. Half a day spent online and on the phone enquiring about electricity prices doesn't sound scintillating, but boy, will it pay for itself. Make a date to do it, rather than keep putting it off. If you're online (there are some great websites to help) you can do it in the evening after work. So put it in your diary for an evening next week. Hell, why not do it this week and save even more?

And use a broker or comparison website for house and car insurance – they'll shop around for good deals and should search every year at renewal time to see if they can get you a cheaper rate if you move.

Sooner or later it will save you money to switch again. Keep checking the competition, and any offers for new customers, and you'll find there's often a saving to make by switching.

Switch off

One of the simplest ways to save money on your electricity and fuel bills is to stop using the stuff. OK, maybe not all the time, but you can certainly turn things on less often.

I rather enjoy the challenge of seeing how late I can go each year before I first turn on the central heating. Of course it depends on the weather, but down here in southwest England I often hold out until 1 November. I find turning it off again in the spring much harder somehow, but I like to turn it off by the beginning of April. In any case, it's only on for a couple of hours morning and evening at the start and end of the winter. An extra jumper or two is enough at those times of year, and gets you into the spirit of frosty mornings and crisp autumn leaves.

Switching off lights sounds obvious too, but it's a habit we often struggle to get into. Perhaps it's easier to start with not switching them on. See how late into the day you can manage without the lights on.

Speaking of lights, those energy-saving bulbs make a big difference. Not only do you save on the bills, but you hardly ever have to change them. I know they cost more to buy, but once you've made the initial outlay (and you don't have to switch the whole house over on the same day) they really pay for themselves.

DON'T HEAT WHAT
YOU DON'T USE

The trouble with central heating is that you're paying to heat all the rooms you're not in, as well as the ones you're using. OK, maybe you keep the radiator turned off in the spare bedroom (if you have one), but no one's going to have the time or the memory to go round every couple of hours, turning radiators on and off, according to who is in the house and what room they're in.

It's much more cost-effective just to heat the room you're in. Leave the central heating off as much of the time as you can, and use electric heaters instead. You'll turn those off when you leave the room, so even if they're theoretically more expensive to run, they work out cheaper. Of course, the whole family ends up in the one warm room, but that can be jolly friendly, and cheery, and sociable.

You may find, depending on where you live, that a wood-burning stove is even more efficient – especially if you have access to free wood for it, either your own or a friendly neighbour's. Where there aren't smoke restrictions you can save a fortune on heating if you install a wood-burner.

Turn it down

Do you know exactly what temperature your hot water is set at? Of course you don't. You do? Grief, have you nothing better to do than check your household appliances on a regular basis? Go and get a life!

Well, whether or not you know what temperature it is, why not just go and turn it down a degree or two? Off you go now, and we'll carry on when you get back.

Well done. That will start saving you pennies straight away. You don't want to turn it down too far, or you'll find you stop adding cold water when you run the bath or shower, or do the washing up, and that would be counter-productive. But a degree or two won't be noticed. And although it sounds like such a little thing, the savings will add up over time – and you can spend them on extra jumpers.

Save water

If your water is metered, you can save a pretty penny by making sure you use less water. Again, this is a habit thing. I've struggled for years to train myself to turn the tap off while I clean my teeth – something I was never taught to do as a child for some reason. I think I've finally cracked it, and the problem wasn't that I thought the tap ought to be on – obviously it doesn't need to be – but simply that I kept forgetting to turn it off. Finally, though, I've reached the point where I instinctively turn it off. And that's where we need to be for many water-saving (and electricity-saving) tactics.

Sometimes it can help to do something in a different way – change your toothpaste, or clean your teeth over the kitchen sink instead of the bathroom basin – just to remind you to think. So try to find ways to get into habits such as putting less water in the bath, or always putting the plug in the kitchen sink instead of holding things under a running tap (ye gods, another one I'm dreadful for).

On top of that there are practical strategies such as putting a brick in the loo cistern, getting 'grey' water (i.e. used bath and sink water) diverted to flush the loos with, collecting rainwater for watering the garden and so on.

If you don't have a water meter, practise all these strategies and, once you're confidently better than me, ask your water supplier to fit a meter.

SAVE PETROL

Goodness knows, petrol is one of the biggest costs these days, especially if you have to use the car a lot. So for a start, you can make sure you're driving the most fuel-efficient car you can. But there are lots of other creative ways to save fuel too:

- *Streamline your journeys.* Why drive home after the school run and then go out to the shops later? Unless the house is right on the route, it's more efficient to shop on the way home. This applies to dozens of other journeys too, of course. You can call in at your mate's on the way home from work to pick up the jacket you left there, instead of driving over there later, and so on.

- *Drive half way and walk the rest.* If you can't drive all the way – maybe the shops or the school or the office are too far – just drive part of the way. If it's a daily weekday trip, even saving two miles a day (that's two one-mile walks, or about 15 minutes each way) will save you 500 miles a year. That's a good bit of fuel. And if you can increase the distance you walk you'll save more money and get fitter.

- *Lift-share to work or school or regular clubs and meetings.* You'll be helping your friends save money too.

Well, that's a start. If you get your brain into gear[1] I'm sure you'll come up with lots more ideas for combining journeys, using your car less and freeing up some of that petrol money for other things. It's another of those things that once you get into the habit requires no effort at all to keep up.

[1] Ha, ha!

Practice
phone
economies

There's a lot of fancy technology around these days, and some of it can really help you keep a lid on your expenses. One of the best of these is VOIP (Voice Over Internet Protocol), which is often known as Skype, although Skype is only one of several examples. Basically it allows you to talk for free over the Internet to anyone else who is also on Skype – all it costs is the price of the headset. And the effort expended in persuading your family and friends to sign up. If you have relatives abroad it can save you a fortune in phone calls, but it will also save you loads on your weekly call to your sister or your best friend just a hundred miles away.

When it comes to the phone, mobiles eat money in a scary way. If you're inclined to overuse yours, always use a pay-as-you-go phone and set yourself a firm budget, and stick to it. See if you can spend less each week or month than you did the one before – the challenge might inspire you to keep those calls down. Or compete with your partner to see who can spend the least (so long as that won't lead to huge rows).

DO YOUR
OWN

One of my friends tells me that she saved £128 a month by getting rid of her cleaner. I can't help feeling sorry for the cleaner, who presumably lost £128 a month, but hopefully she'll have found another job pretty quickly – good cleaners generally do.

Anyway, it's a lot of money, and even if you only cut down the cleaner's hours you can spend a lot less. Maybe you don't have a cleaner, but is there anything you're paying someone else to do that you could do yourself? Cleaning the windows? Ironing? Mowing the lawn? Cutting your hair? OK, you might not want to let your best friend loose on your precious locks, but you get the drift.

Of course, now you need to get the cleaning done. Maybe everyone can share the jobs, kids included if you have them (and if you haven't, there won't be so much cleaning to do). You could even pay the kids (at a much lower rate than your old cleaner). Or you and a friend can clean each other's houses – it's more fun and means you set aside time to get it done or you'd be letting them down. Or you and your friend could both clean your house and then theirs – having company can make it more fun. Or, of course, you can forget all that and just roll up your sleeves and get stuck in.

DIY

One of the most frustrating drains on your finances can come when things break down around the house. It's doubly infuriating because repairing it isn't exciting or fun, like spending money on clothes, or good food, or an evening out. The second the thing is fixed you'll start taking it for granted again.

One of the best things you can do is to brush up on your DIY skills. You don't want to be paying someone else to do a job you should be able to manage yourself. And on top of that, here are a few other ways to keep the DIY costs down:

- *Make it a rule to tackle things* as soon as they start to go wrong rather than waiting for them to fail completely. It's generally much cheaper.
- *Prevention is better than cure* – check things like gutters, car oil, water and so on before problems arise.
- *Keep all the equipment* that comes from flat-pack furniture, old shelves you've taken down, etc. – you never know when that Allen key or those bolts will come in handy.

MAKE
PRESENTS

Sounds awful, doesn't it? All arts and craftsy. Conjures up visions of sitting at the kitchen table (as if you've nothing better to do) surrounded by bits of felt, and coloured cardboard and glue. Well, I can tell you, if that was what it entailed, I certainly wouldn't be advocating it.[1]

---

[1] No offence if you're an arts-and-craftser, and please don't write in. But it is an acquired taste. And trust me that if you saw the standard of my craftwork you wouldn't want it.

What you have to do is to work out what you're good at, and then give gifts you can make really well, rather than ones that are going to turn out mediocre at best. If you can cook, that's great. Fruit cakes, biscuits, toffee, fudge – you're on to a winner here. Or maybe you're a keen gardener? Start early and pot up some seedlings, or plant a few bulbs in a pot. The trick with these presents is to dress them up attractively – a pretty ribbon here, a judicious bow there – so that the overall impression is that it looks special.

If you can't cook or garden, there are other things you can consider. How about tokens that can be exchanged for your time dog walking or cleaning the car? Or downloading some useful freeware from the Internet that the recipient would never have tracked down on their own? Or simply put together a few small gifts in a hamper or attractive box, beautifully packaged in straw or tissue paper – the point being that you can stretch a small budget much further this way.

One way or another, there are things you can do that fall into the category of 'homemade' and which will be really appreciated, while costing you far less than you'd have spent in the shops. And there's something really satisfying about doing it too.

GET THE KIDS
TO MAKE
PRESENTS

Suppose, just suppose, that you read the last section and thought, 'That's really not me. There's no way I'd give anyone anything homemade for Christmas or birthday.' Or maybe you just have limited time. Well, if you have kids, you can still adapt the idea so that you don't have to spend even more on their behalf. Sure, once they're teenagers you might insist they spend their own money on presents, but I don't think that will wash with the little ones.

Now you can, of course, go back to the felt and coloured cardboard creations here. The only trouble is that while the recipient may value them for the child's input, they probably won't value them for much else. If you have a very artistic child, that's a different matter. But with most kids it doesn't really work.

Your best bet is food. The kids will love cooking it, and at Christmas you can pick something that can be cooked in advance and will keep so you can make the gifts before you get stuck into stuffing turkeys and filling mince pies. If your kids are very small, why not make the things yourself and just get the kids to decorate them? It will make for a much quieter life, and the kids will be happy, trust me. And it doesn't really matter how professional the icing or decorating is if the basic food is well made.

Just tell me what relative wouldn't love a box of biscuits iced by little Johnny, or homemade chocolate truffles hand-rolled in icing sugar and cocoa by Millie? Just watch the toffees with grandma's teeth …

Agree a budget

It can be tricky knowing just how much to spend on some people. You don't want to overstretch your finances, but then again you don't want to appear mean or stingy (actually I know some people who seem quite happy to appear tight-fisted, but I imagine if you were one of them you wouldn't be reading this).

The simplest thing to do is to get in touch in advance and agree a budget, especially at Christmas when the presents are reciprocated – well in advance if they're hyper-organised, but a couple of days ahead will probably do fine with others, who still won't have bought your present by Christmas Eve. Most people will be happy to agree in principle but, if you've initiated the suggestion, they may well reply, 'That's a good idea. What sort of budget did you have in mind?' So be ready with an answer to this question. You want to look generous enough without being too generous.

You could, of course, canvas a few friends or family about what would be a reasonable budget to set. Pick ones in a similar gift-budget range. Then whatever amount they say (assuming you can afford it), you reply, 'That's pretty much what I was thinking. Hey, do you fancy having the same arrangement between us?'

HAVE A
FAMILY DRAW

I f the rest of your family are short of cash – or even just short of time – they may well agree to this suggestion. You put the names of everyone in the family into a hat, and then each person draws out one name and buys a present for that person. So Mum might end up buying a present for daughter-in-law, who is buying one for Granddad and so on.

You can, of course, introduce any variations of your choice into this. For example, you can give and receive as couples instead of individuals, if you like. And personally I'd leave the kids out of it – I know how I'd have felt as a child if I'd been told I was only going to get one present from the whole extended family. And anyway, if you do include them, you'll have to cope with their reaction to the news, and no money's going to be worth that.

Use cheap wrapping paper

N o, not the really thin garish stuff that tears as soon as you look at it. Ugh, horrid! No, I mean find ways of wrapping presents using inexpensive materials. In the past I've wrapped all my Christmas gifts in newspaper (the FT, obviously), brown paper, and even fabric (which, incidentally, is the easiest way to wrap tricky-shaped objects such as table lights, or vases, or chainsaws).

Now you've saved a healthy lump of cash on wrapping paper, you can afford to buy ribbons and bows to garnish your paper with. Or print gold stars all over it or something. Or tie the parcels up with colourful wool (much cheaper than ribbons). Go on, have fun. Be creative. If you're wrapping things in fabric you can either buy cheap calico by the metre (a lot cheaper than wrapping paper) or find offcuts of vintage material or something fancy of the kind.

You see? There are lots of options and I'm sure there's something to suit your taste. You just need to have a good think and wrap your head around it.

Trim your Christmas

I f the cost of Christmas is looking pretty unachievable despite all the homemade gifts and wrapping, you need to do some work on editing down your costs. The simplest way to do this is to reduce the list of people you give presents and/or cards to.

Of course, you can mentally strike off everyone who has irritated you this year. Your sister promised to look after the kids that weekend and then let you down? Right, she's off the list. Baby Johnny was sick on you? Well, he doesn't get a present this year then. That'll teach him.

Then again, perhaps that approach isn't exactly going to spread goodwill at the festive season. There are far better ways of going about it. Here are a few ideas:

- *Think about who is as strapped for cash as you are* – or more so – and suggest that you both skip presents this year. They'll be grateful.

- *Institute a policy* that you stop giving presents to godchildren/nieces/nephews once they reach 18. If the oldest is already 25, make it a policy to stop giving at 25.

- *Start a policy* of sending cards only to people you don't see at Christmas.

- *Send e-cards* instead of paying for physical cards and postage.

There. That's looking more manageable already. With a bit of creative thinking you can cut that list right down. And the great thing is that you don't ever have to reinstate those presents and cards so you've saved yourself money for years to come.

SHOP IN THE
JANUARY SALES

I know this sounds completely mad. And it took my wife a long time to talk me round to this one. But the truth is that if you want to save money, you need to start shopping for Christmas in January.

In particular, you will find the most fantastic bargains on Christmas cards and wrapping paper in January. But you'll find all sorts of other things too that will make great presents for friends and family.

Then keep a lookout all year round for inexpensive gifts, or things on offer, or in the summer sales, so you don't have to do that mad rush Christmas-shopping thing in December where you end up spending whatever it costs to buy something – anything – that your dad or sister-in-law or great auntie Gladys could possibly want.

And while you're at it, you can buy birthday cards when you see them going cheap too. Don't wait for a birthday and then buy whatever you have time to get. When you find somewhere that sells bargain-price cards you like, buy a dozen. It's such a joy, too, when the next birthday comes round to find you've already got it sorted. If you have kids, you can apply the same system to buying presents for all those interminable parties your children keep going to. A handy stock of suitable presents in a cupboard somewhere is not only very convenient but can also save you money if you've been buying them wisely.

Try a
student

How do you feel about guinea pigs?[1] Being one, I mean? There are loads of trainees who need people to practise on, and if you're happy to cooperate you can get cheap or even free treatments and services. This applies to all sorts of things from beauty therapy and massage, through to hairdressing (if you're brave) and even dentistry (if you're *very* brave).

Of course, the treatment may take longer than usual, and in some cases you may need to be less than perfectionist. Mind you, if you ask at your local college of further education or other teaching institutes in your area, you should find really good and thoroughly well-supervised treatments. (Incidentally, if you want free dental treatment at a teaching hospital you'll have to de-register with your own dentist.)

If you want a treatment from a student on a one-year course, they may not be up to it before about January, so massages may be thin on the ground between July and the end of the year. Even when this doesn't apply, you may need to make sure you get your hair cut during term time.

---

[1] I hate them personally. They make me nervous – I can't tell which end is which.

RECYCLE
YOUR KIDS'
CLOTHES

We all grew up with hand-me-downs. I was number five in my family, so all my clothes were thoroughly worn through before I ever got them. Obviously this is a great place to start saving money on your kids' clothes. Nowadays children are more resistant, understandably – I resented my oldest brother for getting new clothes when I never did – so when money is reasonably plentiful we often buy clothes for younger children. But if the money isn't there, we can't do that. However, you can still customise the hand-me-downs for the next child – add funky new buttons or dye the thing to make it different.

And how are you going to get more value from your youngest child's clothes? Well, you can cut trousers down to make shorts, which will extend their life, or crop T-shirts, or cut off the sleeves.

Actually, you can make things fairer for your younger children by putting your oldest in hand-me-downs too. Ask friends and family with older kids if they'll pass on clothes to you, or at least sell them affordably. This is especially useful for things like school uniform, Brownies, and Cubs outfits and so on. You can ask parents of older children, or ask the school or organiser, if they can set up a second-hand scheme.

I know kids don't take kindly to being given other people's clothes, especially if you're passing your trendy teenager their nerdy cousin's cardigans. But once they understand that it's freeing up money to pay for a holiday or a Sky subscription, they'll generally work out which side their bread is buttered.

GET HITCHED
ON A BUDGET

There are several ideas throughout this book for saving up for a special event, which could be your wedding but might also be an anniversary, or special birthday, or whatever. But I'm guessing that if you're going through a dry spell you'll also want to keep the costs down as far as possible. Then again, you don't want to compromise your special day, and why should you? So here are a few tips for keeping the final bill as small as possible:

- *Get friends and family to help* – you're bound to know people who are really good at photography, or have a fancy car you can use, or work at a printers, or are great at making cakes, or arranging flowers or decorating church halls, or making clothes. Rope in everyone you can to minimise on paying profit-making professionals.

- *Use websites* that offer all the stationery you need to customise and print off yourself – not just invitations but also the order of service, menus, place cards and so on.

- *Buy a dress off the rail or second-hand.* After all, you'll probably wear it only once and it's often the single most expensive item after the honeymoon.

- *Find a cheap and original reception venue.* My second wedding reception was a barn dance in my in-laws' real barn, with straw bales instead of chairs and tables. Much more fun than an impersonal hotel – and much cheaper.

- *Buy your own alcohol duty free* on a cheap day trip abroad.

- *Shop around for a honeymoon*, or stay nearer home, or find a friend with a house or apartment they can lend you (or all of the above).

HAVE A
BUDGET
BABY

Most new parents prefer to go out and buy the best of everything for their new baby. And that's all very well if you have the money – you can spend it how you like. But what if you don't have it? Well, although the bad news, as you're well aware, is that children are a huge expense from before they're even born, the good news is that if you can change your mindset to one of thrift, there are loads of ways to have a baby on the cheap:

- *Use eBay, freecycle.org and car boot sales* for everything you possibly can.

- *Put the word out around friends and family* that you'd love to be passed on anything that's no longer needed.

- *Don't buy anything you don't need* – if you can't get it for nothing, go without. This includes almost everything apart from the car seat and nappies. You don't need any toys to begin with (you'll be given loads[1]), nor any of those fancy baby gyms, or electric swing seats, or bedside bottle warmers, or special bags to put baby things in – it's just a bag, for goodness' sake, and any bag will do.

- *Breast rather than bottle feed if you can* – it will save you an absolute fortune with no bottles, milk, sterilisers, etc. to buy.

- *Consider cloth nappies* – even factoring in the washing (which doesn't have to be a boil wash these days) you save over the longer term.

- *Join all the baby clubs you can* for the freebies, vouchers and coupons.

Remember, your baby has never known anything else, so it's not going to complain about getting the thrifty treatment so long as you give it all the real essentials – you know, love and all that stuff.

[1] And so will the baby.

DON'T
GIVE UP

About the biggest part of spending less without being miserable is to change your mindset. You need to think in a different way in order to act in a different way.

One of the most dangerous threats to changing your way of thinking – whether you want to spend less, lose weight, give up smoking, or anything else – is that if it doesn't work straight away you abandon it. It's easy to find yourself thinking 'I can't do this,' or 'I'm never going to rein in my spending,' or 'I was doing so well but after that shopping trip today I've blown it.' All of these can far too easily lead to 'I might as well give up.'

In fact, you *can* do it. Other people can, so obviously you can too. Just because it's hard to begin with, that doesn't mean it won't get easier. Just because you spent more than you'd intended today, it doesn't mean you have to overspend tomorrow.

Every time you slip up you can learn something. So when things don't go as you'd planned, ask yourself, 'What have I learned for next time?' Maybe you've learnt to avoid that particular shop, or not to kid yourself you're safe with a credit card, or that you really do need to set up Skype before you call your mother again. Now you can turn today into a useful and positive one in which you've learnt something you didn't know – or hadn't really taken on board – yesterday. So act on it.

Over time, you will find yourself spending less. And when things ease up financially you'll still be able to make your money go further, so you have more for the things you really want. Whatever happened today, you're succeeding if you can just learn to spend less without being miserable.

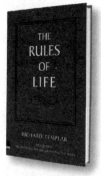

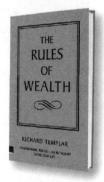